GOD BLESS
the *U.S.A.*
Gift Book

GOD BLESS the *U.S.A.*

Gift Book

Lee Greenwood

PELICAN PUBLISHING COMPANY
Gretna 1992

---

*The word "Pelican" and the depiction of a pelican are trademarks of Pelican
Publishing Company, Inc., and are registered in the U.S. Patent and Trademark
Office.*

Library of Congress Cataloging-in-Publication Data

Greenwood, Lee.
    God bless the U.S.A. gift book / by Lee Greenwood.
      p.   cm.
    A pictorial accompaniment to the words of the author's song "God
bless the U.S.A.".
    ISBN 0-88289-904-X
    1. United States—Pictorial works. I. Title. II. Title: God
bless the USA gift book.
E169.04.G745 1992
973'.022'2—dc20   91-42841
                                                                    CIP

Photo editor Gwen McLin
Cover photo courtesy of Boy Scouts of America

Manufactured in the United States of America
Published by Pelican Publishing Company, Inc.
1101 Monroe Street, Gretna, Louisiana 70053

Introduction

The lyrics contained in this book began as a tiny point of light, but in my heart they burned as bright as the torch in Lady Liberty's hand.

They were written for all Americans, whether born here or not.

They were meant to underscore the promise that America is truly the land of opportunity...

To give hope and spark the smoldering ashes of broken dreams so they can once again become raging fires of success...

And to remind us all that freedom is not free!

The heritage passed on to us can only be protected by our constant vigilance,

Standing guard against erosion from within or attack from those who would take us down because of their envy for what we have.

Besides my right to worship the God of my choice, or to decide whether to worship at all,

The greatest right I have is to say...

I'm proud to be an American!

God bless the U.S.A.!

If tomorrow all the things were gone
I'd worked for all my life,

And I had to start again
With just my children and my wife,

I'd thank my lucky stars
To be living here today,

'Cause the flag still
stands for freedom
And they can't take
that away.

And I'm proud to be an American,
Where at least I know I'm free.

And I won't forget the men who died,
Who gave that right to me.

And I'd gladly stand up next to you,
and defend her still today.

'Cause there ain't no doubt
I love this land...

God bless the U.S.A.

From the lakes of Minnesota,

To the hills of Tennessee,

Across the plains of Texas,

From sea to shining sea,

From Detroit,

Down to Houston,

And New York,

To L.A.,

Well, there's pride in every
    American heart,
And it's time we stand and say...

That I'm proud to be an
    American,
Where at least I know
    I'm free.

*And I won't forget the men
who died,
Who gave that right to me.*

And I'd gladly stand up
next to you,
And defend her still
today.

'Cause there ain't no
doubt
I love this land...

God bless the U.S.A.

Photo Credits

If tomorrow all the things were gone I'd worked for all my life,
And I had to start again—with just my children and my wife,
I'd thank my lucky stars to be living here today,
'Cause the flag still stands for freedom
And they can't take that away.

And I'm proud to be an American,
Where at least I know I'm free.
And I won't forget the men who died,
Who gave that right to me.
And I'd gladly stand up next to you,
and defend her still today.
'Cause there ain't no doubt
I love this land...
God bless the U.S.A.

From the lakes of Minnesota, to the hills of Tennessee,
Across the plains of Texas, from sea to shining sea,
From Detroit down to Houston, and New York to L.A.,
Well, there's pride in every American heart,
And it's time we stand and say...

That I'm proud to be an American,
Where at least I know I'm free.
And I won't forget the men who died,
Who gave that right to me.
And I'd gladly stand up next to you,
And defend her still today.
'Cause there ain't no doubt
I love this land...

God bless the U.S.A.